KNOWLEDGE ENCYCLOPEDIA
SCIENTIFIC & INDUSTRIAL REVOLUTION WORLD HISTORY

© Wonder House Books 2022

All rights reserved. No part of this book may be reproduced or transmitted in any form by any means, electronic or mechanical, including photocopying and recording, or by any information storage and retrieval system except as may be expressly permitted in writing by the publisher.

(An imprint of Prakash Books)

contact@wonderhousebooks.com

Disclaimer: The information contained in this encyclopedia has been collated with inputs from subject experts. All information contained herein is true to the best of the Publisher's knowledge. Maps are only indicative in nature.

ISBN : 9789354401398

Table of Contents

Industrial Revolution	3
An Overflow of Textiles	4–5
Coal & Iron	6
From Iron to Steel	7
Full Steam Ahead	8–9
When Man Made Machines	10
Transportation	11
Railways	12
Roads	13
Cemented Ties	14
An Explosion of Chemicals	15
Advancements in Medicine	16–17
Blowing Glass into an Industry	18
Fossil Fuels: Unlocking New Energy Resources	19
Electricity	20–21
Telegraph	22
Telephone	23
Lighting	24
Banking and Financial Institutions	25
How Industrialisation Was Smuggled Out of Britain	26
Prose During the Industrial Revolution	27
The Industrial Revolution and Poetry	28
The Effect of the Industrial Revolution on Society	29
Pitfalls of the Industrial Revolution	30
Word Check	31–32

INDUSTRIAL REVOLUTION

In Europe, the Agricultural Revolution began in the early 17th century and rapidly progressed in the 18th century. The quantity of crops increased with the use of crop rotation, selective breeding, enclosed fields, new tools, fertilisers, and manure. The new practices and inventions meant people no longer spent most of their time labouring in fields. Nor were so many people needed to farm. Many farmhands, therefore, moved to cities looking for jobs. This marked the start of the Industrial Revolution.

The Industrial Revolution marked the transition from handmade goods to machine-made goods as a result of technological inventions. This period is often referred to as the First Industrial Revolution and was confined to Britain, which by then had become a colonial superpower. Here, advances were made in science and technology, in the fields of iron, steam, textile, and transport. The Second Revolution took place in the late 1850s, when the new inventions of the First Revolution spread to America and Germany. This phase saw immense progress in the steel, electronics, and automobile industries.

This book will chronicle the discoveries and inventions, the inventors, and the progress made in every field, under both the First and the Second Industrial Revolution.

▼ *A Futuristic Vision* is a coloured etching by William Heath that signifies the advancement of technology due to the Industrial Revolution. It led to mechanisation, progress in transport and lavish building projects

An Overflow of Textiles

Textile production was the first to employ the factory system. Before industries began, people produced cotton cloth and woollen goods in their homes, or on a small scale, and it was referred to as a 'cottage industry'. Merchants or traders supplied the raw materials and equipment and returned to pick up the finished goods. But the demand for cotton grew when the upper class began to prefer it. Cotton was the first textile product to undergo mechanisation and mass production. The demand for inexpensive wool and yarn also increased within no time. By the late 18th century, Britain was the world's leading manufacturer of textiles.

▲ *A flying shuttle showing metal capped ends, wheels and a **pirn** of weft thread*

▶ *The original fortified entrance to Richard Arkwright's mill in Derbyshire, Great Britain*

1733
Mechanic John Kay developed the flying shuttle that led to a twofold increase in cloth production. It required four spinners to maintain one loom and ten people to develop yarn for one weaver.

1764
Englishman James Hargreaves invented the spinning jenny (or engine), after his daughter Jenny pushed the family's spinning wheel to the floor, by mistake. James noticed that the **spindle** had not stopped turning. This gave him the idea that one wheel could turn many spindles at the same time. The jenny drew threads from eight spindles.

▶ *Model of the spinning jenny in the Museum of Early Industrialisation, Wuppertal, Germany*

1769
Richard Arkwright patented the water frame—the first automatic spinning machine employing a water wheel. It produced stronger threads than the spinning jenny. The large water frame would not fit in the spinners' homes, so Arkwright built the first modern factory, a water-powered cotton mill next to a stream in Cromford, Derbyshire, England.

1856
William Perkin invented the first synthetic dye. He first called it aniline purple, but later renamed it mauve. Since the dye was cheaper than natural pigments, it was soon applied to cotton fabrics and used by everyone.

◀ *Portrait of Sir William Perkin*

👤 In Real Life

The requirement for **manpower** started reducing in factories with the introduction of machines. Instead of one worker making a piece of fabric, a variety of machines worked simultaneously to produce it. And, instead of only one worker undertaking the entire process of converting the raw wool to dyed fabric, each worker was assigned only one task in the process, following the **assembly-line approach**. This increased the working speed, but performing the same task repeatedly became monotonous for the workers.

WORLD HISTORY | SCIENTIFIC AND INDUSTRIAL REVOLUTION

▲ The only surviving example of a spinning mule built by the inventor Samuel Crompton

▶ Boston Manufacturing Company, 1813–16, Waltham, Massachusetts

1779

British inventor Samuel Crompton merged the features of the jenny and the water frame to create the Crompton's spinning mule. The mule could make both fine and coarse yarn, and one person could operate 1000 spindles at the same time! But Crompton didn't have the funds to **patent** his creation and was cheated by manufacturers. Soon, hundreds of Britain's textile factories were using spinning mules.

1780

English inventor Edmund Cartwright mechanised the process of weaving cloth with a power loom.

◀ Edmund Cartwright

1804

Joseph Marie Jacquard's invention—the Jacquard loom—automatically controlled the **warp and weft** threads on a silk loom.

▶ Portrait of Joseph Marie Jacquard (1752–1834), 1855

1830

The demand for cotton rose so high that the steam engine had to be introduced to speed up the textile industry.

1812

As Britain profited from the cotton production of its American colonies, the cost of producing cotton yarn reduced by nine-tenths. With the **industrialisation** of yarn production, workers who turned wool into yarn were also reduced by four-fifths.

1810

Massachusetts merchant Francis Cabot Lowell memorised the design of the textile machines when he was permitted to tour Britain's factories but not allowed to take notes. Back home, he recreated the designs and started the Boston Manufacturing Company—America's first cloth mill. Several large-scale mills came up in Massachusetts, so this time is considered to be the 'Cradle of the American Industrial Revolution'.

Coal & Iron

Before the Industrial Revolution, Britain, like the rest of Europe, produced coal in a limited quantity because of the small size of coal pits and the abundance of opencast mines (large, open pits dug into the earth). Only local businesses used them. With industrialisation, methods of production improved, and so did the methods of transportation. Fossil fuels like coal, natural gas, and oil became popular, though coal led the way.

The Demand for Coal and the Iron Industry

The iron industry became the major coal user. An English village, Coalbrookdale pioneered iron tramways that helped transport coal to buyers or even within the mines. Iron was used in the construction industry as well as to build coal-operated steam engines. Coal production increased by 50 per cent in 1700–1750, and by the year 1850, it went beyond 500 per cent. It was cheaper than wood and produced three times more energy. As the demand for coal increased, mines were dug deeper and mining became more dangerous. A series of steam-engine innovations helped pump water from the ground and dig deeper for coal. Richard Trevithick built the first moving steam engine in 1801. He believed that a steam engine on rails would be more effective than horse wagons to carry loads of coal and iron to and from the mines.

▲ *View of Coalbrookdale Ironworks, Shropshire, England (1758)*

Coal & Canals

Before 1750, Britain's roads were not smooth and well-connected, and ships were used to transport coal. In 1761, the Duke of Bridgewater inaugurated a **canal** from Worsley to Manchester for carrying coal. The demand for cheaper coal helped expand production and made him rich. Seeing his success, coal-mine owners built other canals.

◀ *Based on John Blenkinsop's patented design, Matthew Murray built a steam locomotive named Salamanca in 1812 for the Middleton Railway to transport coal. It ran between Middleton and Leeds, England*

Coal & Brass

The West Midlands, England, was nicknamed the 'Black Country' because the entire area was covered with black smoke and soot from coal used in iron **foundries**, steel mills, and **furnaces** during the Industrial Revolution. In Birmingham, England, the metal industry boomed with the mass production of buttons, brass fittings, pins, guns, and nails.

Incredible Individuals

In 1700, the iron industry was on a decline and there was a shortage of charcoal. This was solved in 1709 by Abraham Darby, an ironmaster who, having worked with brass, moved to Coalbrookdale, Shropshire, England and purchased a semi-derelict blast furnace. He was the first to use coke—a form of processed coal—to smelt iron. This was a success story as it separated iron from ironstone. In 1715, he opened a second blast furnace. His son Abraham Darby II succeeded him and he learned to make better quality coke by burning coal in ovens and thereby improve the quality of iron. When Darby II died in 1763, his son Abraham Darby III continued the business, and he built a unique bridge above River Severn using iron from his late grandfather's furnace.

From Iron to Steel

With the rapid growth of industries and infrastructure, iron and steel became very important materials and were included in many building and construction processes. In time, steel began to be preferred over iron because it is stronger, though it is also more difficult to produce. Steel came to be used in weapons, transportation, telegraph lines, and buildings.

When Steel Mills Took Over the Landscape

In 1901, the United States Steel Corporation was formed and it was one of the world's largest steel-producing companies at the time. Throughout the 20th century, the scale of steel production increased dramatically for all stages of **infrastructure**. This included constructing large-scale blast furnaces to melt iron ore, open-hearth furnaces, oxygen furnaces, molten steel casting, and port-based mills from where ships transported raw materials and finished goods, as seen in countries like South Korea and Japan. Steel mills were being built close to locations that had huge deposits of coal and iron ore. For instance, such deposits around Birmingham, Alabama, Minnesota, and Michigan led to the construction of steel mills in the Great Lakes region of the United States.

The Rise of Buildings

The steel industry skyrocketed in the late 19th and 20th centuries during the Second Industrial Revolution and vastly transformed America. More and more buildings had to be constructed to accommodate the country's immigrant population. Steel was chosen for the inner skeleton inside stone constructions because it could withstand harsh conditions and was strong enough to support the skyscrapers it was used in.

▶ The US Steel Tower in downtown Pittsburgh

Incredible Individuals

In 1856, British engineer Henry Bessemer invented the first inexpensive process to produce steel on a large scale. The process could turn molten iron into steel within 20 minutes. Soon, Scottish-American industrialist Andrew Carnegie began building steel mills, following the Bessemer technique, to produce steel on a massive scale. Carnegie invested in and produced steel when he realised that the 2,858 kilometres transcontinental railroad from Nebraska to California would require a lot of steel. It was finally completed in 1869.

▲ An illustration of Sir Henry Bessemer

Isn't It Amazing!

William Le Baron Jenney constructed the first skyscraper in 1885 called the Home Insurance Building. It was 138-feet tall and had 10 storeys.

▶ The exterior of the Home Insurance Building in Chicago, USA

Full Steam Ahead

Till the invention of steam engines, the industries had relied on energy harnessed from wind, water, animals such as horses, and manpower to operate small machines. Earlier, wood was burnt to produce fuel. This changed when Britain discovered that it had rich deposits of coal. The steam engine that was built to pump out the water from coal mines later helped run a variety of transport services such as ships, railway **locomotives**, and factories, which vastly improved transportation on land and water.

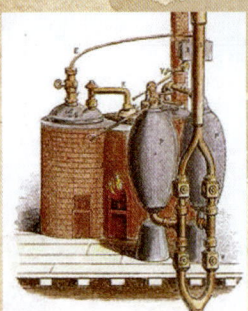

◄ The 1698 Savery Engine

◄ The Newcomen Memorial Engine in Dartmouth

1698

Thomas Savery patented a steam engine that he called the 'miner's friend'; it helped solve problems related to mine drainage and increased the public water supply. It was a pump with hand-operated valves. Steam from a boiler was condensed in a cylinder, creating a **vacuum** that sucked water from the mines into it. By controlling valves, the water was pumped upwards using the same steam. It generated about one **horsepower** (HP), but was ineffective given its short height and vulnerability to boiler explosions.

1712

Englishman Thomas Newcomen's steam engine called Newcomen Atmospheric Machine caused a slight vacuum in the cylinder when cold jets of water condensed the steam. A **piston** was used in the process. The engine was large and used at the bottom of a mine, but it only produced five HP and used up a lot of coal. Still, when he passed away in 1933, 110 engines were found to be operational in France, Germany, Austria, Hungary, and Sweden.

1776

Scottish inventor James Watt altered Newcomen's invention to produce steam. He added a separate condenser to his engine to prevent the heating and cooling of the cylinder. Watt's steam engine could rotate a shaft instead of the simple up-and-down motion of the pump. It generated 5–10 HP. By 1800, his company had built 496 engines that were used to power machinery, locomotives, ships, distilleries, canals, waterworks, paper, flour, cotton, and iron mills.

In Real Life

The first transoceanic voyage to employ steam power was completed in 1819 by *SS Savannah*—an American sailing ship with an auxiliary steam-powered paddle. Crossing the Atlantic at that time was dangerous and the sea captain Moses Rogers initially found it difficult to find a crew for the journey. There were hardly any passengers willing to risk their lives on the first steamship to voyage across the Atlantic Ocean.

The ship sailed from Savannah in Georgia, USA to Liverpool in England, in a little more than 27 days. Being a hybrid sail ship, the *SS Savannah* used a lot of steam power during the day, but also depended on traditional sail power for its journey. By the second half of the 19th century, larger and faster steamships were regularly carrying passengers, cargo, and mail across the North Atlantic, a service dubbed 'the Atlantic Ferry'.

▲ A steam engine built as per James Watt's patent in 1848 at Freiberg, Germany

WORLD HISTORY | SCIENTIFIC AND INDUSTRIAL REVOLUTION

British engineer Richard Trevithick built the first railway steam locomotive—the Penydarren locomotive—which undertook its first journey on 21 February 1804. Its 5 wagons carried 10 tons of iron and 70 men, and it travelled at a speed of 3.9 kmph (2.4 mph).

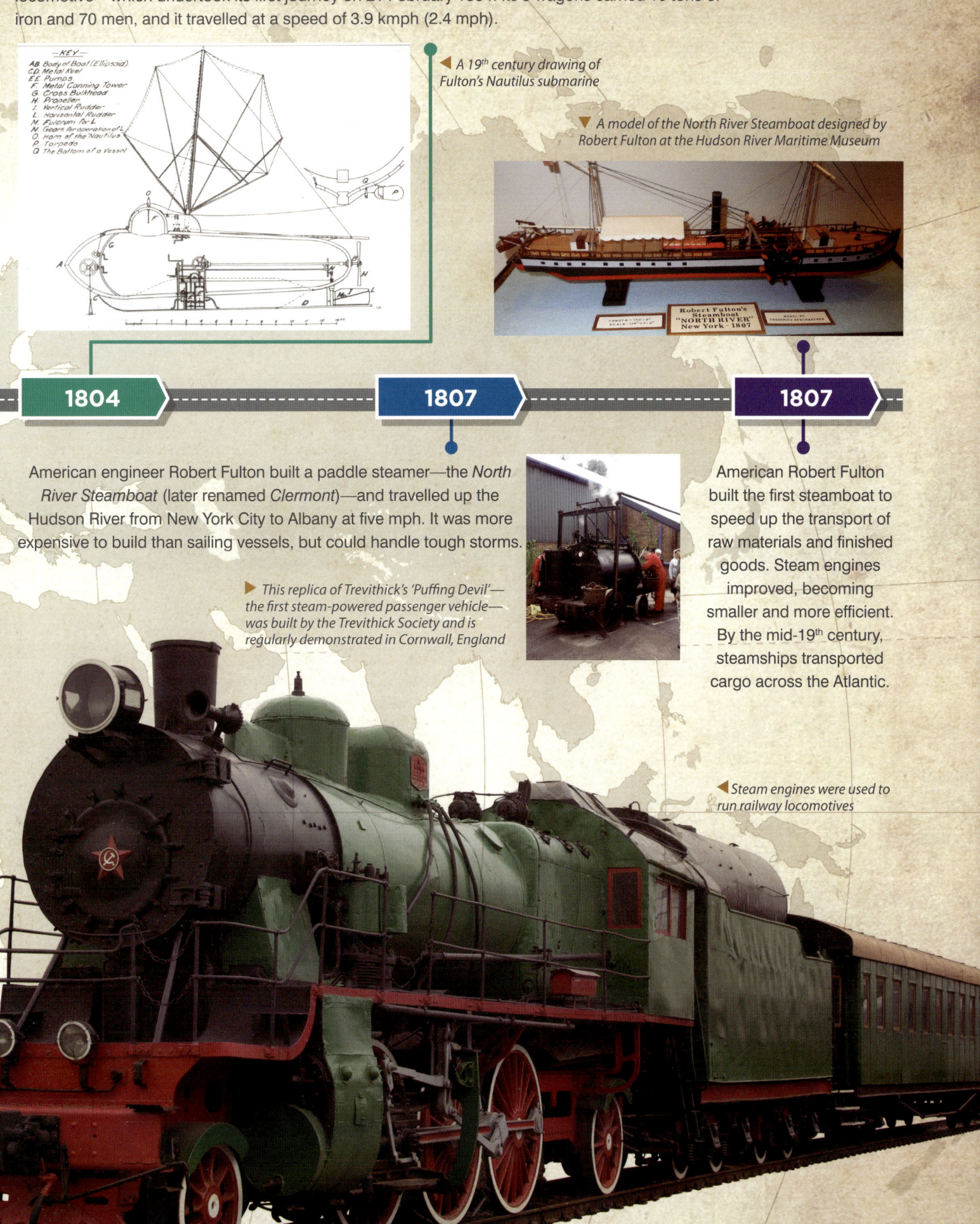

◀ A 19th century drawing of Fulton's Nautilus submarine

▼ A model of the North River Steamboat designed by Robert Fulton at the Hudson River Maritime Museum

1804

American engineer Robert Fulton built a paddle steamer—the *North River Steamboat* (later renamed *Clermont*)—and travelled up the Hudson River from New York City to Albany at five mph. It was more expensive to build than sailing vessels, but could handle tough storms.

▶ This replica of Trevithick's 'Puffing Devil'—the first steam-powered passenger vehicle—was built by the Trevithick Society and is regularly demonstrated in Cornwall, England

1807

American Robert Fulton built the first steamboat to speed up the transport of raw materials and finished goods. Steam engines improved, becoming smaller and more efficient. By the mid-19th century, steamships transported cargo across the Atlantic.

1807

◀ Steam engines were used to run railway locomotives

When Man Made Machines

Machine tools used in the production of manufacturing machines were important during the Industrial Revolution. They were originally developed in the 18th century as tools for clock, watch and for scientific-instrument makers to produce small, precise mechanisms in batches. These small mechanisms, when used in textile machines, were called 'clockwork' because of their metal gears and spindles. Birmingham, in 1830s England, is an example of how manufacturing changed because of machine tools. A new machine by William Joseph Gillott, William Mitchell, and James Stephen Perry helped mass-produce sturdy and cost-effective steel nibs (points) for dip-writing pens. The production of these items used to be taxing and costly.

▲ In 1827, English pen-maker Joseph Gillott started Joseph Gillott's, a company based in Birmingham, England to produce dip pens

Growth of Bigger Machines

The early models of machines used very little metal because they were manually shaped with files, saws, hammers, chisels and scrapers. But after the Industrial Revolution, machine tools were used to make small metal parts and frames. Production of large machine parts was a problem till the cylinder **boring machine** was designed for steam engines. At the start of the 19th century, the **slotting machine** was developed and then the milling machine, which only gained prominence during the Second Industrial Revolution.

▲ Universal Milling Machine

▲ A slotting machine, built in 1863 in Netherlands, delivered to the Nagasaki Steel Mill

⭐ Incredible Individuals

Henry Maudslay, one of the famous toolmakers of the early 19th century, was responsible for training many engineers, toolmakers, and inventors of the next generation. During his stint at the Royal Arsenal, Woolwich, he saw large horse-driven wooden machines. He later worked for Joseph Bramah on the production of metal locks and machinery for ships' pulley blocks required by the Royal Navy at Portsmouth Block Mills, England. His workshops welcomed inventors like Sir Joseph Whitworth, Richard Roberts, James Nasmyth and Joseph Clement. Roberts made high-quality machine tools and encouraged the use of **jigs** and gauges for precision in workshop measurements.

▲ Albert Edward, Prince of Wales, and Princess Alexandra at Gillott's Victoria Works in 1874

▲ The bust of Henry Maudslay, a renowned tool maker of the 19th century

Transportation

The internal-combustion engine and the gasoline-powered automobile changed the face of transportation. Automobiles replaced the horse-and-carriage mode of transport and offered far greater mobility to the public.

Building Infrastructure to Improve Transport

The increase in the trading of goods and services, a result of rapid industrialisation, instantly improved Britain's transport pathways. This created many jobs. Engineers were called in to construct more tunnels and bridges, and find more routes. The creation of railroads led to an increase in the demand for coal and fuel to construct locomotives, and iron was required to build railtracks. For instance, by 1815, Britain had around 2,000 miles of functional canals; and by 1840, the US had over 3,000 miles of railroad tracks.

The Evolution of Automobiles

In 1859, Belgian inventor Étienne Lenoir constructed a working model of an internal combustion engine that mixed coal gas and air. In 1878, German engineer Nikolaus Otto tweaked the model into a four-stroke cycle comprising induction, compression, firing, and exhaust. Otto's models came to be used instead of steam engines. In the early 1890s, German engineer Rudolf Diesel used heavy oil, or diesel, in his engine as it was more efficient. His diesel engines were used in submarines, locomotives and heavy machinery. In 1885, the first motorcycle and motorcar by Daimler and Karl Benz used the gasoline-powered engine. Within two decades, American industrialist Henry Ford mass-produced automobiles, including his famous Model T, which was reliable and efficient. Mass production helped slash the prices of his automobiles and made them affordable to the average-income earning American.

▲ *Rudolf Diesel (1858–1913). His engines were so effective that it is speculated that he was killed by coal barons, who stood to lose a lot of money, when he went missing on a ship. His body was found on the shore a few days later*

▶ *Otto's 1876 four-cycle engine*

In Real Life

It was found that cities situated near railroads prospered economically, compared to those away from the rail route. Factories began to thrive because a routine had been formed—finished goods were being transported from factory doorsteps to the markets, daily. Raw materials too were being transported from the markets to the factories, every day. Many companies only worked to build and operate railways. In time, large railway companies purchased the smaller ones and kept growing in the process.

◀ *The last home of Karl and Bertha Benz, now the location of the Gottlieb Daimler and Karl Benz Foundation in Ladenburg, in Baden-Württemberg*

Railways

The 1790s and 1800s were known for 'Canal Mania' as canal-building began and Britain invested a lot of money in building these waterways. By 1850, Britain had about 4,000 miles of canals. These helped transport coal, which was in high demand, from mines to factories. Horse-driven wagons were used to reach the waterways. The wagons were fitted with a steam engine to help push them over inclines, but this was rather a slow process. Then, in the 1840s, 'Railway Mania' began. Railroad construction in America boomed from the 1830s to the 1870s. European countries too followed Britain in building railroads (Belgium in 1834, France in 1842, Switzerland in 1847, and Germany in the 1850s). Perishable goods such as dairy products could now be transported across long distances without getting spoilt.

Landmark Moves in the Growth of Railways

In 1767, Richard Reynolds made a wooden set of rails for transporting coal from Coalbrookdale. The first act to create a 'railway' was passed by parliament in 1801. Till this point, horse-driven carts were used to pull coal. Then, in 1801, Richard Trevithick developed the first steam locomotive to be driven on roads. George Stephenson built the first steam-hauled public railway, the Stockton to Darlington railway, hoping to derail the monopoly of the canal owners, in the year 1821. The 40 kilometre long railroad connected coal mines at Shildon in North England to nearby towns, and to Stockton and Darlington.

▲ Trevithick's No. 14 engine was built around 1804 by an ironworks company, Hazledine and Company, in Bridgnorth. It can be viewed at the Science Museum (London) today

▲ Portrait of British engineer Richard Trevithick

In Real Life

White-collar workers moved out of cities and went to live in the suburbs because it was now possible to commute back and forth. Working-class districts were demolished for new rail buildings. In 1844, the British government passed a law stating that third-class accommodation would be allowed on at least one train a day travelling in each direction. The fare for each of these third-class passengers was not to exceed a penny for each mile travelled.

Stiff Competition From Canals

The Bridgewater Canal's owner initially opposed the building of a railway at Manchester, nonetheless the Liverpool and Manchester Railway opened in 1830. Seeing great potential for future passenger travel, the railways gradually created a permanent staff. In the same year, major railway lines were installed to connect big cities and towns. Canal companies rose to the challenge and reduced their prices, but industrialists sided with the railways, and from 1835–48 there was a massive boom in the creation of railways. In fact, a standardised time was introduced across the country so that trains could be timetabled, making Britain one of the first few countries to do so.

◄ The development of railways not only brought about a monumental shift in trade and industry, but also helped connect people better

▲ The Bridgewater Canal, famous for its commercial success, crossing the Manchester Ship Canal, is one of the last canals to be built

Roads

Before industrialisation, British roads were the decayed remains of what the Romans had built over a millennium and a half ago. Then, Mary I, also known as Queen Mary Tudor, passed a law stating parishes would be in-charge of improving their own roads using the assistance of workers six days a week, for free, and landowners had to provide the equipment. Unfortunately, the workers were not well-trained and didn't do much to restore the roads.

Legislation after 1750

Due to Britain's industrial expansion and population growth, the government passed laws to stop the road system from decaying any further, but it did not improve it in anyway. The Broad Wheel Act of 1753 widened the wheels on vehicles, and the General Highway Act of 1767 adjusted the sizes of the wheels and the number of horses per carriage. In 1776, a law was passed for parishes to employ men specifically to repair roads.

Improved Quality of Roads

By 1800, the quality of roads improved. Stagecoaches became so frequent that they had their own timetables. In 1784, the Royal Mail was introduced and its coaches delivered the post across Britain. While various industries used them, roads played only a small role in moving freight—a task that canals and railways did efficiently. Roads, however, played an important part in transporting goods (and people) once they came off the railways and canals.

Isn't It Amazing!

The British road system introduced Turnpike Trusts—organisations that took care of a few sections on the road and charged every traveller a toll. The first turnpike (toll road) was created in 1663, on the Great North Road (now A1), and the first actual trust was formed in 1703 by the parliament. While many turnpikes worked towards improving the speed and quality of travel, some trusts for turnpikes kept all the money and did nothing to improve the conditions of the roads. As turnpikes covered only a fifth of the British road network, local transport did not benefit much, and, in fact, some parish roads were better maintained. However, wheeled transport expanded under the reign of turnpikes.

▲ A road marker post built by the Turnpike Trust in Bath, England

▲ An oil painting of the Edinburgh and London Royal Mail, by Jacques-Laurent Agasse

Cemented Ties

Building lighthouses to prevent shoreline accidents involving warships and merchant ships became necessary for Britain, a naval superpower. For this, it needed a binding agent that could hold tall structures. In the 1700s, engineers experimenting with limestone discovered a powder that, when wet, would set and hold stone blocks together. This was cement.

Experiments in Cement

In the year 1757, engineer John Smeaton observed that good quality lime had a high amount of clay. Two years later, while building the third Eddystone Lighthouse at the Cornwall coast in Southwestern England, Smeaton found that mixing leftover clay, lime, and crushed **slag** from the iron-making process created a mortar that became hard when left to set under water. Smeaton's discovery motivated builders in England to come up with better quality cement.

British bricklayer-turned-builder Joseph Aspdin created a new type of cement in 1824 by firing clay and limestone till they calcined. He patented this cement and called it Portland cement because the concrete it produced looked very similar to the Portland stone that was often used to construct buildings in England. Portland cement became so popular that famous English engineer Marc Isambard Brunel used it to construct the Thames Tunnel in 1843. Two years later, Isaac Johnson improved the cement's quality by firing a mixture of chalk and clay at close to 1400° C–1500° C, which is what is used today.

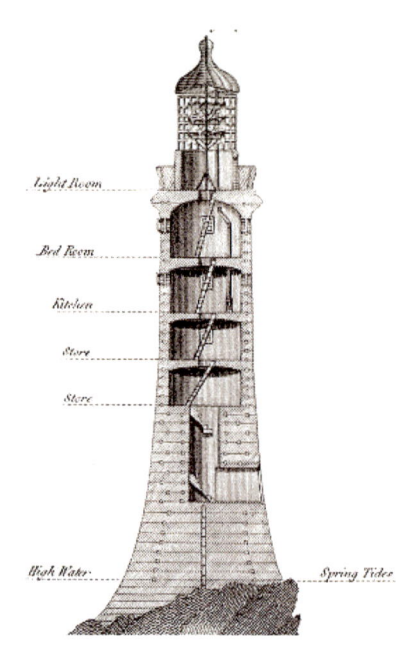

▲ *A contemporary engraving of the lighthouse by engineer John Smeaton on the Eddystone Reef*

◀ *A blue plaque about Joseph Aspdin at Packhorse Yard in Leeds, England*

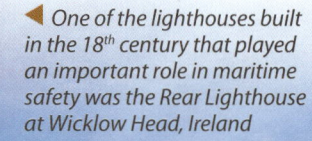

◀ *One of the lighthouses built in the 18th century that played an important role in maritime safety was the Rear Lighthouse at Wicklow Head, Ireland*

 Isn't It Amazing!

A ship carrying barrels of Aspdin's cement—named after the man who, some say, created a **prototype** of the first artificial cement—sank near the Isle of Sheppey in Kent, England. The barrels were found with cement set in them. After removing the wooden staves, these were given to a pub in Sheerness, England, where they can be admired even today.

WORLD HISTORY | SCIENTIFIC AND INDUSTRIAL REVOLUTION

An Explosion of Chemicals

The chemical industry saw the invention and large-scale production of chemicals right from the start of the Industrial Revolution. In 1635, John Winthrop Jr. became the first to open a chemical company in Boston to produce potassium nitrate. A century later, a series of inventions made chemical manufacturing a booming industry.

It Began with Sulphuric acid

Pharmacist Joshua Ward was the first to heat saltpetre and allow the sulphur to combine and oxidise with water to produce sulphuric acid in 1736. Englishman John Roebuck (James Watt's first partner) ensured large-scale production of the chemical in 1749 by establishing a big factory in Prestonpans. Sulphuric acid was used to bleach cloth and pickle (remove rust from) iron and steel. Roebuck increased his manufacturing by replacing costly glass vessels with bigger, cost-effective chambers made using riveted sheets of lead, later called leaden condensing chambers. Then, in 1791, Nicolas Leblanc patented the Leblanc process—the production of sodium carbonate (synthetic soda ash) from sea salt (sodium chloride)—which also created a lot of harmful wastes like hydrochloric acid and sodium sulphate. The chemical was used in the glass, textile, soap, and paper industries.

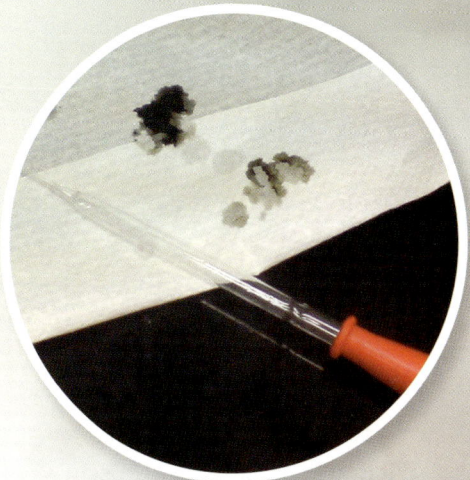
▲ Drops of 98 per cent sulphuric acid instantly char a piece of tissue paper. Carbon left as a residue from the dehydration reaction stains the paper black

Chemistry Takes Off

In 1800, Scottish chemist Charles Tennant created bleaching powder (calcium hypochlorite), based on French chemist Claude Louis Berthollet's discoveries that drastically reduced the process time from months to days. In 1855, Benjamin Silliman, from New Haven, Connecticut, obtained gasoline, naphthalene, tar, and other solvents by distilling petroleum. The first commercial oil well specifically drilled for oil was near Titusville, Pennsylvania, in 1859.

In 1888, chemical engineering was introduced as an undergraduate programme of four years, called Course X, and was taught at the Massachusetts Institute of Technology (MIT) in the United States. It was a combined course of mechanical engineering and industrial chemistry, training students to solve problems in engineering, especially those related to the use and manufacture of chemicals and their products.

In 1918, Fritz Haber received the Nobel Prize for the synthesis of ammonia, which German chemist Carl Bosh put to commercial use in 1930.

▲ An 1830 illustration of the cylinder furnace used in Leblanc's process of soda production

In Real Life

Before the Industrial Revolution, **greenhouse gases** like carbon dioxide (CO_2) and methane (CH_4) always remained at around 280 parts per million (ppm) and 790 parts per billion (ppb). Today, the concentrations are about 390 ppm and above 1,770 ppb respectively. Increasing levels of these gases are responsible for global warming and climate changes. Their increase is attributed to human activities that rely on fossil-fuel combustion, which causes an increase in emissions of these gases. The Industrial Revolution and subsequent industrialisation increased such emissions manifold.

▲ Fritz Haber (1868–1934)

▲ A plaque at the site where Charles Tennant's St. Rollox Chemical Works was originally located

Advancements in Medicine

Before the Industrial Revolution, bacterial (plague), viral (smallpox), and waterborne diseases (cholera, typhoid, and typhus) wiped out large chunks of the population. As **urbanisation** and industrialisation increased and the populations in cities grew, so did slums and poverty. The living and working conditions of the people worsened and there were further outbreaks of disease. However, the Industrial Revolution also brought many scientific breakthroughs in modern medicine. It improved the production of stethoscopes, scalpels, microscope lenses, test tubes, etc., and introduced **vaccines**, new cures, and treatments.

English doctor Edward Jenner discovered the cure for smallpox, which had been causing death and sickness since the 3rd century BCE. He observed that milkmaids who contracted cowpox did not contract smallpox after **variolation**.

▲ *A stethoscope of the French physician René Theophile Laennec, who devised the first stethoscope in 1816. The brass and wood model consists of a single hollow tube*

1772

Joseph Priestly discovered nitrous oxide (NO_2). Later, Sir Humphrey Davy used it to numb the body parts on which surgery was to be conducted. From the 1930s onwards, it was also used to relieve the pain experienced during childbirth.

1776

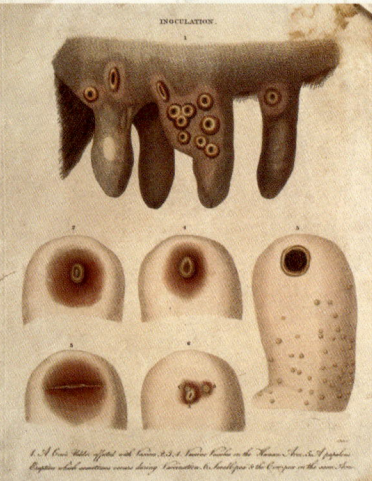

◀ *A coloured engraving done in 1811 by J. Pass, showing vaccinia pustules on a cow's udder as well as a smallpox and cowpox pustules on human arms*

1816

René Laennec invented the stethoscope. Before this invention, physicians had to put their ear on the patient's chest, used to be awkward for both the parties, and even produced inaccuracies in diagnosis as the internal sounds were muffled.

1897

British doctor Ronald Ross won the Nobel Prize for his discovery of a parasite in the gastrointestinal tract of a mosquito, linking malaria to the insect.

◀ *A record of 'pigmented bodies' in mosquitoes on a page from Ronald Ross's notebook. The bodies were later identified as malaria parasites*

1895

Axel Cappelen performed the first open-heart surgery at Rikshospitalet (now Oslo) on a man who had been stabbed and was bleeding from his coronary artery.

1895

Wilhelm Röntgen identified X-rays after he found a new ray that could pass through many substances and leave a 'shadow' for anything solid, like bones. Six months later, X-rays were used to locate and remove bullets from the bodies of wounded soldiers.

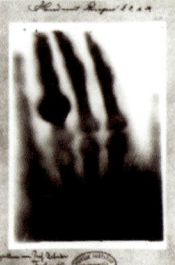

▶ *Handmit Ringen (Hand with Rings) is a print of an X-ray taken by Wilhelm Röntgen. One of the first of its kind, it is an X-ray of his wife Anna Bertha Ludwig's left hand*

WORLD HISTORY — SCIENTIFIC AND INDUSTRIAL REVOLUTION

Isn't It Amazing!

Lady Mary Montagu was an English aristocrat, writer, and poet. She's often thought to have saved more lives than any other human. She brought smallpox inoculation practices from Turkey to Western medicine. Her actions led to the eradication of small pox. She is also credited for saving around 500 million lives in the 20th century alone.

▼ James Blundell

▶ Lady Mary Montagu

1818
British obstetrician James Blundell conducted the first successful human blood **transfusion** on a patient who had **haemorrhaged** during childbirth. Later, in 1901, Austrian physician Karl Landsteiner established blood groups.

1829
French chemist Charles Henri Leroux first isolated the 'miracle drug' salicylic acid (proto-aspirin). In 1853, Charles Frederic Gerhardt added an acetyl group to it and created acetylsalicylic acid (true aspirin). German chemist Felix Hoffmann developed it into the tablet form to mitigate fevers, headaches, common cold, and muscle aches. In 1899, the German company Bayer finally named it aspirin.

1845
English physician and pathologist John Hughes Bennet was the first to describe leukaemia as a blood disorder. Later, Franz Neumann linked the disease to bone marrow, and by 1900, experts connected it to a list of disorders.

1884
Jaume Ferrán y Clúa created a live vaccine that he had isolated from cholera patients in Marseilles. Later, Waldemar Haffkine developed a cholera vaccine with milder side effects.

▲ Waldemar Haffkine

1867
Joseph Lister, often referred to as the 'Father of Antiseptic Surgery', promoted cleanliness, antiseptic surgical methods, and carbolic acid to clean wounds and instruments as the vital elements in a patient's speedy recovery.

1847
Charles Babbage devised the ophthalmoscope that was popularised by Hermann von Helmholtz in 1851, and perfected by Greek ophthalmologist Andreas Anagnostakis soon after. This mechanism provided a magnified image of the patient's eye to the clinician.

◀ The brain of Charles Babbage, called the 'Father of Modern Computing', displayed at the Science Museum, in London

Blowing Glass into an Industry

The pace of glassmaking increased in 1635 when Sir Robert Maxwell began to use coal instead of wood, and glass industries no longer had to be based in forest areas. Several technological advancements from Germany and England brought glass production up to a level where it could be called an 'industry'.

Noteworthy Inventions in Glass

In 1851, one of the earliest uses of glass in structures was at the Crystal Palace for the Great Exhibition in London, where 3,00,000 glass panes were used as panels. Around 1900, American inventor Michael Owens created the automatic bottle-blowing machine that produced 2,500 bottles per hour. In 1923, the gob feeder was developed to supply consistently sized gobs in bottle production. Then, in 1925, the IS (Individual Section) machine was developed to work with gob feeders. The combination of an IS machine with the gob feeder that produces many bottles in one go is the crux of most automatic glass-container production today.

▲ A print of a photograph of the Owens Automatic Bottle Machine with ten arms. Each arm of the machine was fitted with bottle-making moulds. The fully automatic machine produced bottles faster and with different capacities

Float Glass

In the 1960s, Sir Alastair Pilkington's 'float' method of glassmaking was a revolution in the glass industry. He was looking for a more economical way of making high-quality glass that could be used for mirrors, shop windows, cars, and other applications where the requirement was distortion-free glass. The success of the Pilkington's method is based upon the careful balance of the volume of glass fed onto the bath, where it is flattened according to its height. Sir Alastair Pilkington's float glass method is used by 90 per cent of flat glass manufacturers even today.

▲ An engraved crystal vase by Gallé, circa 1900

Incredible Individuals

Over 1890-1920, **art nouveau** had a profound impact on glass art. Popular artists designing art nouveau glasses were Emile Gallé (France), Josef Hoffman (Austria), Louis Comfort Tiffany (USA), Joseph Maria Olbrich (Austria) and Karl Koepping (Germany). Early French glassmakers drew inspiration from Gallé for his 'pate de verre' enamelling technique, which involved firing coloured glass to create translucent surfaces of different colours. Others worked with a thick, clear glass pressed into **moulds**, to trap bubbles in a 'verresouffle' or 'bubble glass technique', or highlight relief surfaces (a type of sculpture).

▲ Emile Galle's self-portrait

Fossil Fuels: Unlocking New Energy Resources

Even before the potential of coal was discovered during the Industrial Revolution, oil and natural gas had long been in use, largely as a fuel for lamps and as grease for vehicles and equipment.

The Oil Industry

In 1853, one of the first oil wells was drilled in a forest near Bóbrka, Poland. In the same year, Ignacy Lukasiewicz, a Polish pharmacist and a rock-oil mine owner, was the first to distil kerosene from oil; he also invented the kerosene lamp. It was found that although steam engines were efficient, they were slow starters, quite costly and could only be produced in small numbers. Petroleum-based fuel didn't have all these drawbacks. Moreover, the mass production of automobiles in the early 20th century increased the demand for petrol, and this fuelled the oil industry.

▲ The Lucas Oil Gusher at Spindletop Hill (an oil field), South of Beaumont, Texas, USA

▲ Bóbrka is an important landmark in the history of the oil industry

▼ A gas torch on an oil field

In Real Life

Carbon, apart from being released through evaporation, soil erosion, and volcanos, is stored below the ground in the form of fossil fuels and soil. It balances the Earth's 'carbon budget'. But that balance was disrupted during industrialisation, when fossil fuels were extracted on a large scale to produce energy and fuel. Their continued and increasing use has caused pollution of air, water, and climate.

Incredible Individuals

It was a merchant, John Austin, who introduced kerosene to the USA. He noticed a cost-effective oil lamp while travelling in Austria, and produced an upgraded version of it in the USA. This led to a boom in the country's rock-oil industry, as the prices of whale oil had already escalated because of the decrease in the number of these mammals. Suddenly, oil prices collapsed as production and refining increased. In 1859, an entrepreneur, Samuel Downer Jr. patented 'kerosene' as a trading name and put a licence on its use.

Electricity

The first reference to static electricity can be traced back to 600 BCE when ancient Greek philosopher Thales recorded that light materials were attracted to rubbed amber. He called materials like amber, glass, etc., 'electricks' after the Greek word for amber, 'elecktron'. Later, acclaimed 16th century physicist William Gilbert became the first to use the phrase 'electric force'.

The next notable landmark was German scientist Otto von Guericke's invention of the first electric generator in the mid-17th century. By the Second Industrial Revolution, electric power surpassed steam in its use. The pioneers of electricity were plenty and their inventions transformed the lives of generations to come.

Pioneers of Electricity

In 1752, the man who gave America its constitution, Benjamin Franklin, tried to collect electricity from lightning by flying a kite near thunderclouds. The kite was attached to a conductive wire; and to the wet kite string, a silk ribbon was tied along with a metal key that was connected to a Leyden jar. When Franklin moved his hand near the key, he got a shock. This led to the realisation that lightning could be diverted to the ground to prevent it from causing casualties.

▲ An artist's depiction of Benjamin Franklin flying a kite in an attempt to collect electricity from lightning

Discovery of Voltage

In 1799, Alessandro Volta gave the world the concept of Volt (symbol: V), the unit of measurement for electromotive force. He came up with it while inventing the electric battery. Belgian Zénobe Gramme conceived the dynamo, also called magneto, which was the first generator, in 1868. In the same year, the first hydroelectric power station became operational in Switzerland, and in 1891, the first high-voltage line was built between Lauffen and Frankfurt in Germany. Simultaneously, between the 19th and 20th centuries, Serbian-American engineer Nikola Tesla invented alternating-current (AC) motors, generators, and transformers as well as the Tesla coil used in radios, televisions, and other electronic equipment.

▲ Nikola Tesla (1856–1943) was one of the greatest scientific minds that the Earth has ever seen. An engineer, for whom money was not the primary goal, who would have changed the world if his Wardenclyffe project had come into being. Instead, he sadly died alone, penniless, and with only pigeons for friends

▲ Nikola Tesla's AC dynamo-electric machine (AC electric generator) in the 1888 US Patent 390,721

The Making of the Electrical Generator

In 1831, British scientist Michael Faraday successfully passed an electric current through a wire coil between two magnet poles, and by the next year, an electrical generator was built on this principle. This was a crucial step in our understanding of electromagnetism.

▲ One of Faraday's 1831 experiments demonstrating induction. The liquid battery (right) sends an electric current through the small coil (A). When it is moved in or out of the large coil (B), its magnetic field induces a momentary voltage in the coil, which is detected by the galvanometer

▲ Michael Faraday (1791-1867) came from a very poor family, but became one of the greatest scientists of history. It is even more impressive given that during his time science could only be pursued by those with enough wealth to support the education and resources that accompany scientific exploration

Another important discovery was the Ohm's Law, used to measure electrical current, in 1927 by Georg Simon Ohm. This eventually became the basis of the electric motor and the electric generator or dynamo.

▶ Georg Simon Ohm

▼ Nowadays, steel lattice transmission towers connect overhead power cables across electrical grids

In Real Life

The Electricity Fairy is an enormous mural (10 x 60 m) painted by Raoul Dufy for the 1937 World's Fair in Paris. Now installed at the Paris Museum of Modern Art, it describes the history of electricity and its modern applications and has portraits of around 100 famous scientists and inventors who contributed to the development of electricity.

▲ A caricature of Sir Hiram Stevens Maxim called In the Clouds. He was the chief engineer of the United States Electric Lighting Company in 1878, where he discovered a method of manufacturing carbon filaments

Telegraph

The electric telegraph was the first electronic mode of communication that improved the delivery of letters. Prior to this, the Pony Express (a continuous relay of men on horseback delivering the mail) was the go-to mode of communication, and it would take 10 days to deliver a letter from Sacramento to Missouri.

Inventions before the Electric Telegraph

In 1809, Samuel Soemmering first invented a raw model of the electric telegraph, in Bavaria. He used 35 wires (for each encoded character) with a gold electrode placed in water. This way, messages could be read till 2000 feet away, and interpreted depending on the amount of gas bubbles produced by electrolysis.

▶ *A sketch of Soemmering's electric telegraph*

Early Telegraphs

In 1828, Harrison Dyar invented the first telegraph in the USA, where the chemically treated paper tape would undergo electrical sparks to produce a coded message of dots and dashes. In 1837, British physicists William Fothergill Cooke and Charles Wheatstone patented the Cooke and Wheatstone 'needle' telegraph (the receiver had a number of needles that electromagnetic coils moved to point to letters on a board).

◀ *William Fothergill Cooke and Charles Wheatstone's electric telegraph (needle telegraph) from 1837, now in the Science Museum, London*

▲ *Charles Wheatstone and William Fothergill Cooke*

Incredible Individuals

Morse invented an electric telegraph system that was a great success. He built upon scientist Joseph Henry's discovery that electromagnets could be used to send a 'message' over a long distance. By 1835, he proved that signals could be **transmitted** by wire. His mechanism could move a marker to write codes on a paper strip, and soon emboss paper with dots and dashes. This is how the Morse code was born. On 1 May 1844, the first news transmitted over Morse's line was the nomination of Henry Clay from the Whig Party. It was carried by hand to the Annapolis Junction, between Washington and Baltimore, and wired to the capital by Morse's partner Alfred Vail. On 24 May 1944, Morse let Annie Ellsworth, the daughter of a friend, dispatch the famous message "What hath God wrought?" from a *Bible* verse, from the old US Supreme Court chamber, to his partner in Baltimore to officially declare that the line was completed.

▲ *Samuel Morse (1791-1872)*

▲ *A Morse code receiver and recorder that dates back to the late 19th century*

Telephone

Till 1877, the telegraph was the only reliable source of long-distance communication. In the same year, several scientists were working on a new and effective way of communicating over long distances—the telephone. Alexander Graham Bell, who began his research in 1874, managed to win the first US patent for the telephone in 1876.

By 1879, the telephone had grown so popular that Western Union and the telephone system reached an agreement to operate as two separate services. Earlier in 1853, French professor Édouard-Léon Scott de Martinville, who was also a teacher of the deaf and mute, thought about 'electronic speech' and invented the phonautograph, which recognised the vibrations of speech.

▲ An illustration of French professor Édouard-Léon Scott de Martinville's phonautograph

Father of the Telephone

The phonautograph and the telegraph both inspired the Scottish inventor Alexander Graham Bell to invent the telephone. On June 2, 1875, along with assistant electrician Thomas Watson, he observed that when the reed moved in a **magnetic** field, the frequencies and tone of spoken sound waves could be reproduced. On March 10, 1876, Bell spoke into the receiver of the instrument to Watson, who was in the other room with another telephone, saying the famous words, "Mr. Watson—come here—I want to see you." This invention instantly lowered the demand for telegraphs as 'talking with electricity' was faster and more exciting. Bell went on to own the American Telephone and Telegraph Company (AT&T).

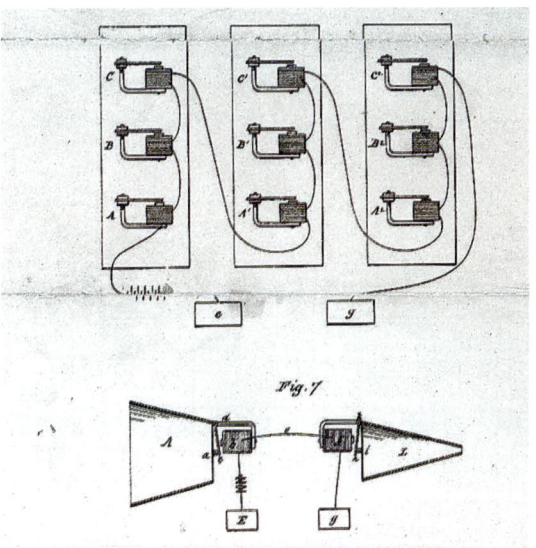
▲ A patent drawing of Alexander Graham Bell's telephone. It was the first instrument that could transmit human speech through a machine

Other Notable Inventions

While Bell patented the telephone first, American inventor Elisha Grey had also created prototypes of the same. The two inventors fought a long battle over taking credit, but Bell won. In 1849, Italian immigrant Antonio Meucci designed the telephone and, in 1871, even filed a caveat to announce his invention. Unfortunately, Meucci could not afford to renew the caveat and so his contribution to the discovery was not considered. But on 11 June 2002, the United States House of Representatives honoured Meucci's inventions.

▲ Antonio Meucci, photographed by L Alman

Isn't It Amazing!

In 1888, Bell invented an advanced version of Thomas Edison's phonograph. Edison, in turn, invented the microphone that could be fitted into the telephone. People no longer had to scream into the receiver to be heard at the other end.

▲ Alexander Graham Bell on the telephone, calling from New York to Chicago in 1892

Lighting

Gas and kerosene lamps were the only source of artificial lighting till the early part of the Industrial Revolution, but their popularity declined in the next 50 years, after the invention of the electric light bulb during 1878–79.

A Tussle Between Gas Lighting & Electricity

Gaslight technology evolved in England in the 1790s, and by 1879 people had grown used to the idea of lighting with gas. Gaslight manufacturers started to provide better quality gas and brighter lights. Besides, they had existing infrastructure, while electric lighting required power-generating plants to be built with connecting wires across the entire distance. Edison decided to design his electric lighting system based on the model of the gaslight technology. But, unlike the manually operated gas lamps, Edison's electric lighting system was automatic. Then in 1880 came Sir Hiram Maxim's lamp which contained a high-resistance **filament**. It was produced quicker than usual because Maxim hired Edison's expert glassblower, Ludwig Boehm. The United States Electric Lighting Company used the Maxim lamp in their installed electric lighting systems for many years.

▶ A gas lamp being manually lit on a street in Stockholm. Can you imagine how difficult it must have been to light up an entire city using such lamps?

Incredible Individuals

The electric bulb underwent many inventions. Between 1878–79, an English inventor, Joseph Wilson Swan, and an American, Thomas Alva Edison, both invented an incandescent lamp. They were engaged in a long tiff till they agreed to form a joint company called Edison & Swan United Company in 1883. Swan got patents for many features of the lamp before Edison, but since the latter conceived power lines and other lighting equipment, he is given more credit. In 1886, inventors Elihu Thomson and Edwin Houston jointly began manufacturing incandescent lamps under Sawyer-Man patents. In 1892, J. Pierpont Morgan orchestrated a merger between Edison and Thomson-Houston, and together they formed General Electric.

▲ Thomas Edison's first successful light bulb model, used in a public demonstration at Menlo Park, December 1879

▲ Thomas Alva Edison's portrait

▲ Inside Thomas Edison's Menlo Park Laboratory

Banking and Financial Institutions

The three banking tiers in existence at that point in England comprised the Central Bank of England established in 1694, 30 private banks preferred by traders and industrialists, and 12 county banks. Prior to 1750, copper was used for daily transactions, and gold and silver for major ones. Commercial bills and paper money too were in existence. By 1750, private banks kept growing, in terms of both status and business.

Development of the Banking system

Increasing business opportunities and the resultant wealth brought with them the need to deposit the earnings in one place, and also acquire loans for building equipment and infrastructure for factories, railways and canals. This gave rise to specialist banks that catered to certain industries. The merchants supplied some of the circulated capital. Some of it came from the **aristocrats**, who had acquired money from land and estates and were now keen on increasing their wealth by investing it and assisting others. They were able to supply land, capital and infrastructure.

By 1800, England had 70 private banks and 24 county banks. But the Napoleonic Wars scared the public and led to a mass withdrawal of money, till the government passed a rule stating that only paper notes, not gold, could be withdrawn. The Country Bankers Act of 1826 put a limit on the issuance of notes, and many banks had to make their own notes. This resulted in the formation of joint-stock companies. The end of the 19th century saw the merger of many localised banks.

▲ An illustration of the interior of the Central Bank during working hours in the 1800s

Incredible Individuals

The finance sector produced a group of individuals from the Midlands called 'shock troops' who inadvertently helped spread the revolution by buying land with their profits. These were managers, capitalists, merchants, financiers, and salespersons, who ranged from key figures to small-scale players in the finance industry.

▼ The Bank of England gained a monopoly over the issue of banknotes with the Bank Charter Act of 1844

How Industrialisation Was Smuggled Out of Britain

Britain tried hard to keep the benefits of industrialisation to its home shores so it could dominate the global economy and trade. But visiting Europeans and Americans who had learnt the secrets and techniques of creating machines went back to their countries and reproduced factories and railroads. At times, the machines were even smuggled out of Britain in rowboats to other countries. The first few countries to follow Britain's lead were France, Belgium, Germany, and Switzerland.

Outside Europe

The American Civil War (1861–65) was an 'industrial war' where the urban, industrially advanced people of the Northern states fought the agriculturally inclined people in the Southern states that used slave labour. As a result, both sides reacted differently to the Industrial Revolution. Industrialisation continued despite the war, and by 1900 USA was producing 24 per cent of the world's output in manufacturing, overtaking Britain. In 1870, the **monarchy** in Japan adapted quickly to early industrialisation. But in Russia, the czar and the nobility struggled with the harmonious implementation of industrialisation. Industrialised nations, with the help of their armies and naval forces, were able to colonise countries that were not at par with them, and exploited these colonies for raw materials which they used in their own factories.

▲ Crew members of the ship USS Wissahickson standing beside a Dahlgren XI-inch pivot gun during the 1863 American Civil War

Incredible Individuals

In 1789, Samuel Slater took industrialisation to American soil when he **migrated** from Britain to Rhode Island, USA. He built the first textile factory there, purely from memory, as British authorities would have seized any written notes. Between 1810–12, Francis Cabot Lowell returned to Massachusetts after a trip to England and set up the first power loom that merged mechanical spinning and weaving in the USA.

▲ Located on the banks of the Blackstone River in the United States, the historic Slater Mill used water-powered machines to spin cotton

▲ Samuel Slater (1768–1835) is popularly called 'The Father of the American Industrial Revolution'

Prose During the Industrial Revolution

Many authors were influenced by the Industrial Revolution and wrote stories based on the lives of working-class people and the oppression and injustices they experienced in industrial England. A new genre of writing known as the 'industrial novel' emerged, it dealt with the lives of the workers. Authors used their works to portray how, although on the surface society looked like it was progressing, the poor and working classes experienced severe hardships. Child labour was common in factories and mines, moreover the working conditions were in such a dismal state that it often put their lives at high risk. Authors contributed to bring about change by highlighting the plight of this particular strata, eventually the society and government took notice and worked towards their upliftment; laws were passed and changes were made to improve the lives of the working class as well as of women and children.

▲ An illustration from the novel North and South by Elizabeth Gaskell

Charles Dickens

In his famous classic *Oliver Twist*, English author Charles Dickens depicted the harsh living conditions during this time in history. *The Pickwick Papers, Hard Times, A Christmas Carol,* and *David Copperfield* are some of his works that reflect his own experiences while working at a blacking factory. His works justly portrays the horrid conditions of the working class in the light of his own experiences. He openly wrote about the treatment of children across England. His stories focus on social injustices and upon people whose life was ravaged by poverty during the Industrial Revolution.

Elizabeth Gaskell

She was a famous female author from the mid-1800s. Belonging to England's Manchester—a city that was an industrial powerhouse known for its cotton—she wrote *North and South*. In the novel she covered the plight of the working class, poverty, and other social issues during the Industrial Revolution. Her novel *Mary Barton* is about the struggles of a working-class family. She received a lot of criticism because she openly sympathised with the working class.

In Real Life

Robert Owen was a businessman and social reformer from New Lanark, Scotland. In the early 19th century, he managed a cotton mill which became a model community. He worked hard for the rights and upliftment of the working class. His famous work, *A New View of Society* focused on his principles of educational philanthropy.

▲ Robert Owen (1771-1858)

The Industrial Revolution and Poetry

Child labour, the plight of the working class, the destruction of nature, etc., were some of the consequences of the Industrial Revolution that led many poets like William Blake, Percy Shelley, John Keats, and William Wordsworth to criticise the revolution. Some of them felt that it had caused more harm than good, and they called upon the people of Great Britain to remember the times when industrialisation and urbanisation had not spread across the country.

▲ An extract from the poem The Chimney Sweeper by William Blake

 ## William Blake

Labour laws prevalent at the time of the Industrial Revolution allowed children to work. They were discriminated against and paid much lower wages than those received by adults. They had to work for long hours and some of them even began working as early as age four. William Blake's poem, *The Chimney Sweeper*, from his collection *Songs of Innocence and Experience*, is about the injustice suffered by child chimney sweeps. Blake explains the sad lives of innocent children who, on the pretext of their small size, were forced to climb up the chimney's and clean them.

 ## William Wordsworth

Industrialisation lead to an increase in the number of factories, and the need for more labour. Many people moved to the cities for jobs. But the workers were underpaid and lived in small houses with poor living conditions. They no longer lived near nature but in polluted cities. William Wordsworth was a poet famous for his love for nature. Although the Industrial Revolution did solve some problems, he felt that it violated the relationship between humans and the environment in many ways. In response to the effect of the Industrial Revolution on nature, William Wordsworth, in his poem *Lines Composed a Few Miles Above Tintern Abbey*, recalls happier times spent in nature as compared to the lonely rooms and din of towns and cities.

In Real Life

Caroline Norton (1808–1877) was a poet who wrote about the issue of child labour, and through her poems such as *A Voice from the Factories* spoke about the harsh conditions and suffering of the children working in factories at the time of the Industrial Revolution.

▲ Caroline Norton

▲ A portrait of the English poet William Wordsworth

The Effect of the Industrial Revolution on Society

Industrialisation and urbanisation led to increased demands for greater social welfare, labour rights, education, equality, and political rights. In 1807, the African slave trade was abolished in America. In 1832, the British Great Reform Act was passed, which saw the representation of the manufacturing cities of Birmingham and Manchester for the first time, causing a change in the organisation of the parliament and governance.

Industrialisation Changed all Sectors

Industrialisation had increased the production of coal by twentyfold, 'pig' (crude) iron by thirtyfold and textiles by fifteenfold. There was development in the iron, textile, transportation, banking, and communication industries. The number and variety of manufactured goods increased, they became more affordable and were easily available to the masses. The standard of living for middle and upper classes improved. The **oligarchical** ownership that initially controlled the means of production encouraged a bigger distribution of ownership through common stocks. Britain's working-class' conditions improved by the end of the 19th century as the government passed various labour reforms, including the workers' right to form trade unions.

▲ *Iron and Coal by William Bell Scott illustrates the rise of coal and ironworkers in the Industrial Revolution and the complex engineering projects they made possible*

More Spending Power

The costs of clothes, tools, and household items reduced due to mass production. Employment opportunities rose as new factories were constructed and the need for manpower required to operate the machines increased. Factory employees earned more than farmers. People were no longer dependent on their farms for income. The growing middle class now had access to economic power that, till now, was held by aristocrats.

Isn't It Amazing!

The Great Exhibition in London, 1851, was testimony to the progress Britain had made with industrialisation. On display were revolvers, telegraphs, reaping machines, sewing machines, and steam hammers to showcase how the British were the world's best manufacturers of machinery.

The Rise of Specialist Professions

Industrialisation led to a change in the nature of work as well as manufacturing, and encouraged specialisation. Teachers and trainers were hired to impart specialised skills. Workers were divided into groups. Some had to transport raw materials such as coal, iron and steel. Some handled the functions of different machines, others repaired them, and still others upgraded or improved their efficiency. Work was divided in this manner and each department gained expertise in particular areas. Specialised departments handled **sanitation**, traffic, and taxation. The significance of specialised professionals such as lawyers, builders, physicians, and others increased as well.

Pitfalls of the Industrial Revolution

While the Industrial Revolution was known to have heralded rapid growth and change while improved the quality of life in Britain, America, and several other countries, it also had its **drawbacks.** While it brought large profits to the upper classes, it also led to subhuman living and working conditions for the working class that often lacked even basic **amenities**.

Decreased Quality of Life

Young children were employed for long hours in dangerous environs at very low salaries by textile mills and factories. In the early 1860s, one-fifth of Britain's textile industry had workers younger than 15 years of age. Factory workers had to toil 14–16 hours per day, 6 times a week. Men earned twice the amount women did, and children earned even lower. The working conditions, especially in the mines, were dangerous. Unskilled workers had no job security. Machines replaced craftspeople. Most machines were dirty, produced soot and smoke, and their use caused many ailments and accidents resulting in death and injuries.

Poor Work and Housing Infrastructure

Alongside modern buildings, inferior low-cost housing options such as shanties and shacks also cropped up. Better wages attracted migrants to industrial cities and towns, but these places were unable to tide the flow and number of new workers from the countryside. Local sewerage and sanitation systems took a toll. This—along with overcrowded homes, pollution, and unsanitary living conditions—caused a number of disease outbreaks such as smallpox, cholera, typhus, and tuberculosis.

▲ *Michael Sadler was a British historian and educationist. He led the factory reform movement in England and worked to regulate and improve factory conditions and working hours, especially for children*

Rise in Obesity

Use of tractors, trains and automobiles certainly made life easy. With the rise of automation, various professions became **sedentary** and the invention of the TV and the radio gave rise to 'couch potato' culture. This way of life has led to an array of lifestyle diseases including obesity, diabetes, and hypertension.

▲ *A 19th-century representation of the cholera epidemic. Cholera, an unknown disease in the Western Hemisphere before 1830, turned out to be one of the most feared diseases of the 19th century*

Root Cause of Environmental Threats

Most of the world's current environmental problems began or were exacerbated during the Industrial Revolution. Depletion of Earth's natural resources such as water, trees, soil, rocks, and minerals, fossil fuels, etc., began with the Industrial Revolution. While coal was responsible for kick-starting the Industrial Revolution and changing the way people utilised energy, it eventually had an ill-effect on the environment and, in turn, the health of all living beings. Air and water pollution, loss of flora and fauna, and global warming are considered to be the ghastly after-effects of industrialisation. Before 1750, atmospheric carbon dioxide existed in concentrations of 275 to 290 parts per million by volume (ppmv). It had crossed 400 ppmv by 2017.

Word Check

Amenities: Desirable or useful features or facilities of a building or place.

Aristocrats: A social class of the highest order in society, it often consists of the nobility and people who hold ranks and titles.

Art nouveau: A new style of art that began around the year 1890 and spread through Europe and the USA. It was often used in architecture, design, etc., and was based on the idea of art being a part of daily life and applying art to everyday objects.

Assembly-line approach: It refers to a process where a line of workers or machines complete a specific job on a product as it is being produced or built. The production process is divided into steps, and no single worker or machine completes the entire task.

Boring machine: A machine with a cutting tool that is used to either make a smooth and accurate hole, or to enlarge a hole that has already been drilled in a material.

Canal: Artificial waterway or man-made channel of water to allow transport of goods and services.

Factory: A space that produces goods and services using machines operated by trained staff.

Filament: A thread or conducting wire with a high melting point at the centre of an electric bulb or thermionic valve that gets heated by an electric current.

Foundries: Workshops or factories for casting metal.

Furnace: Closed area where materials can be heated at very high temperatures to harden objects.

Greenhouse gases: Gases that trap the Sun's energy and cause warming of Earth's surface, also known as the greenhouse effect.

Haemorrhage: When blood escapes from a damaged blood vessel

Horsepower: A unit of power that measures the rate at which a device performs mechanical work

Industrialisation: The development of industries in a country or region on a wide scale

Infrastructure: Man-made structures (e.g. buildings, roads, power supplies) that assist in the functioning of a society

Jig: A special device that holds a work piece and guides the machine tool as the operation is carried out

Locomotive: A powered (usually electric or diesel) railway vehicle used for pulling trains

Machine tools: These are power-driven tools used to cut, drill or fashion metals or other hard materials into useful parts

Magnetism: A physical phenomenon produced by the motion of electric charge, which results in attractive and repulsive forces between objects

Manpower: The total number of people working on a project or for an employer

Manufacturing machines: These are machines used to create or assemble items (like cars), with little or no help from humans

Migration: Relocating or moving to a new place, usually for job opportunities

Monarchy: A form of governance where the monarch (ruler/king/queen) rules the land till death; power is then transferred to the monarch's heirs

Moulding: A piece of wood or other material fitted as a decorative architectural feature

Oligarchical: A small group controlling the affairs of a country or organisation

Oxidiser: A chemical with which a fuel burns

Patent: An exclusive right to a product or process given to the inventor (an individual or a firm), which permits the manufacture, use or sale of the invention and excludes others from doing so, usually for a limited period of time

Pirn: A rod-like device similar to a reel or spool on which weavers wind thread for weaving

Piston: A disc or a piece of solid metal that is part of an engine and moves back and forth inside a cylinder to press a liquid or a gas into a small space to impart or derive motion

Prototype: The original version of a product from which the final version is developed. It is mostly created during the testing and evaluation phase and is found to lack a few features that the final product has.

Revolution: A drastic change in the way a system/organisation/country works; the change can be for the better or worse, and can be sudden, temporary or ranging over a long period.

Sanitation: Public health conditions, including provisions for clean drinking water and disposal of human excreta and sewage

Sedentary: Sitting most of the time, somewhat inactive

Slag: Stony waste matter that is separated from metals during the process of smelting or refining ore

Slotting machine: A machine with a tool that moves up and down and is used to cut slots and grooves of different sizes in materials

Spindle: A straight wooden spike used for spinning and twisting fibres of wool, flax, hemp, and cotton into yarn

Static electricity: An electric charge caused by friction

Transfusion: The process of transferring blood from one human being into the circulatory system of another human of the same blood type

Transmission: The process of broadcasting or transferring something from one person or medium to another

Urbanisation: The process by which large numbers of people shift from living in the countryside to towns and cities.

Vaccination: Administration of a vaccine to the body to build immunity or strength to fight off a particular disease

Vacuum: A space entirely devoid of matter

Variolation: A method of immunising patients against smallpox by infecting them with a mild form of the disease (using a substance taken from the pustules of patients). It is no longer in use.

Warp: It is a term used to describe the direction of threads in a fabric. These threads run vertically, parallel to the selvedge (fabric's edge).

Weft: It is a term used to describe the direction of threads in a fabric. These are the threads that run perpendicular to the selvedge.